I0797802

When we are born,
we are blessed with
gifts.

It will take time to
discover...

LOYOLA PRESS.
www.loyolapress.com

Authors: Pope Francis and Paul A. Reynolds
with Peter H. Reynolds

Editor: Gary Jansen

All illustrations: Peter H. Reynolds

ISBN: 978-0-8294-6158-9

Published in Chicago, IL
Printed in the United States of America

25 26 27 28 29 30 31 32 33 34 CGC 10 9 8 7 6 5 4 3 2 1

Our Treasures Within

POPE FRANCIS
PETER H. REYNOLDS
WITH PAUL A. REYNOLDS

LOYOLA PRESS.

A Message from

POPE FRANCIS

All of you have a chest, a box, and inside
there is a treasure. Your job is to open the chest, discover
the treasure, develop it, give it to others and receive
from others the treasures they offer.

If we keep it there, closed up, it will stay there.
If we share it with others, the treasure will multiply
– along with the treasures that come from others.
What I want to say is don't hide the treasure
that all of you have.

Sometimes you find it right away.
But sometimes it's like playing a treasure hunt,
because it is not found easily.
Once you find it, share it.

We are ALL gifted.

Each one of us
has treasures within.

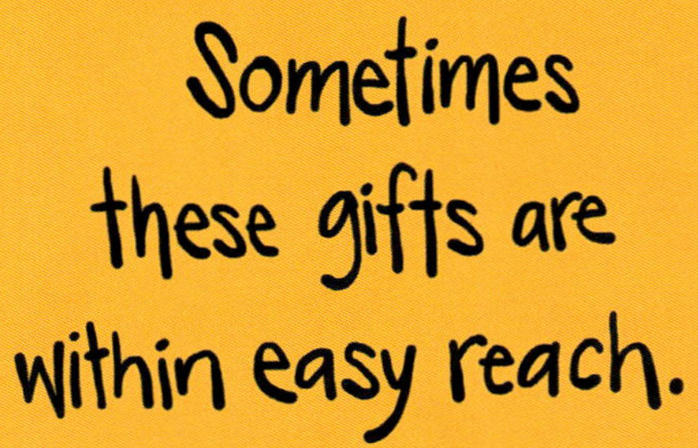

Sometimes
these gifts are
within easy reach.

But sometimes they
are deep inside waiting
to be discovered.

Some discover the
gift of song –

Their voices
filling the air with
music from the heart.

Others find their
gift of art –
bringing joy and beauty
to the world.

And some people
reach within and find
the gift of words...

...weaving stories
that inspire, comfort,
and help us dream.

And some people
find they have
a special gift
for deep listening.

Truly hearing others.
Understanding them—
making them feel seen.

The gift of kindness is in there too
– waiting to be put into action.

A warm smile.

A small act that can
change someone's whole day.

And, of course,
the greatest gift?

The gift of love.

And what do we
do with our gifts?

We share them!

A song is
to be heard.

A story is
to be told.

A kind word is to be spoken.

An act of love can heal and transform.

And when we

share our gifts

something **wonderful** happens.

They grow.

The more we give
the more the world
fills with light.

So...
what are
your gifts
and how will you
share them?

The world is waiting.

share the treasures that you were blessed with . . .

A Message from PETER and PAUL

Growing up, we had the good fortune of crossing paths with members of the Jesuit community – the same order to which Pope Francis belonged. In particular, it was Father Bernardo (John) Bonowitz – who was both a Jesuit, and eventually a Trappist monk – who gently mentored us in the spirit of Ignatian spirituality. It deeply shaped how we see the world and our role in it.

At the heart of Ignatian teaching is the call to discern one's gifts, talents, strengths, and creativity, and to use them in service of others – to help create a more compassionate, just, and beautiful world. That message has become a guiding light in our life's work.

And so, it is an incredible honor to help bring Pope Francis' words to life through this picture book – inspired by a conversation he had with a group of young people in 2015. His enduring message is one of love, hope, and purpose – offered in a way that invites young hearts and minds to reflect, dream, and make their mark. When Pope Francis passed away on April 21, 2025, we felt called to continue this project, which had been in development since early 2023.

It is a joy to be able to share it now and to play a small part in ensuring Pope Francis' messages will continue to inspire youth around the world —and the grown-ups who care for them—for generations to come.

Blessed to share the treasures within – with you,

Peter Paul

Peter H. Reynolds
Paul A. Reynolds

Fr. Bonowitz is greeted by Pope Francis at the Vatican during a papal audience with Cistercian superiors.

Dedicated to

Our dear friend and mentor,
Father Bernardo (John) Bonowitz, OSCO
originally a Jesuit and then a Trappist monk
who served as Abbot in Brazil, and who helped us
understand the power of discerning our talents,
creativity, and gifts— and using those gifts to
move the world to a better place.

PHR & PAR

"All of you have a box,
like a treasure chest with
a treasure inside.
And the word for you is to
open up the chest, take out the treasure,
make it grow and give it to others,
and receive from others
the treasure
that other people have."

—Pope Francis